FAVORITE BRA

RIVAL
Crock&Pot®

The Original and #1 Brand Slow Cooker

Publications International, Ltd.

Favorite Brand Name Recipes at www.fbnr.com

Preparation/Cooking Times: Preparation times are based on the approximate amount of time required to assemble the recipe before cooking, baking, chilling or serving. These times include preparation steps such as measuring, chopping and mixing. The fact that some preparations and cooking can be done simultaneously is taken into account. Preparation of optional ingredients and serving suggestions is not included.

CONTENTS

CROCK-POT® SLOW

Stirring

Due to the nature of slow cooking, there is no need to stir the food unless the recipe method says to do so. In fact, taking the lid off to stir food causes the slow cooker to lose a significant amount of heat, which extends the cooking time required. Therefore, it is best not to remove the lid for stirring.

Adding Ingredients at the End of the Cooking Time

Certain ingredients are best added toward the end of the cooking time. These include:
• Milk, sour cream and yogurt: Add during last 15 minutes.
• Seafood and fish: Add during last 60 minutes.
• Fresh herbs: Fresh herbs such as basil will turn black with long cooking, so if you want colorful fresh herbs, add them during the last 15 minutes of cooking time.

Pasta and Rice

For best results with rice, always use long-grain converted rice. Most recipes suggest adding pasta or rice halfway through the cooking time for best texture. If rice doesn't seem completely cooked after the suggested time, you may add an extra ½ cup to 1 cup of liquid per cup of rice, and extend the cooking time by 30 to 60 minutes.

Cooking with Frozen Foods

You may cook frozen foods in your **CROCK-POT®** slow cooker. However, it is best to use the following guidelines:
• Add at least 1 cup of warm or hot liquid to the stoneware before placing frozen meat in the slow cooker.
• Do not preheat the unit.
• Cook recipes containing frozen meats for an additional 4 to 6 hours on LOW or 2 hours on HIGH.

Cooking Temperatures and Food Safety

Cooking meats in your **CROCK-POT®** slow cooker is perfectly safe. According to the U.S. Department of Agriculture, bacteria in food is killed at a temperature of 165°F. Meats cooked in the **CROCK-POT®** slow cooker reach an internal temperature of 170°F in beef and as high as 190°F in poultry. It is important to follow the recommended cooking times and to keep the cover on your slow cooker during the cooking process to maintain food-safe temperatures.

Browning Meat

Meat will not brown as it would if it were cooked in a skillet or oven at high temperatures. It is not necessary to brown meat before slow cooking; however, if you prefer the flavor and look of browned meat, just brown it in a large skillet sprayed with nonstick cooking oil. Place the browned ingredients in the stoneware and follow the recipe as written.

COOKER Hints and Tips

Herbs and Spices

When cooking with your **CROCK-POT**® slow cooker, you may use whole herbs and spices rather than crushed or ground. The flavor and aroma of crushed or ground herbs may lessen during the extended cooking time with the slow cooker. Be sure to taste and add more seasonings, if needed. If you prefer colorful fresh herbs, add them during the last 15 minutes of cooking time.

Making Breads and Cakes

Here are some tips on making delicious desserts and baked goods:

- Do not over-beat the batters of breads and cakes. Follow all recommended mixing times.
- Do not add water to the **CROCK-POT**® slow cooker unless instructed to do so in the recipe.
- After breads and cakes have finished cooking, allow them to cool in the stoneware for 5 minutes before removing them.

The breads and cakes in this recipe collection may be prepared in the stoneware; however, you may wish to use the **CROCK-POT**® Bread 'N Cake Pan for best results. You may purchase one by calling 1-800-577-4825 or going online to www.crock-pot.com.

Cooking for Larger Quantity Yields

When preparing recipes in a larger unit, such as a 5-, 6-, or 7-quart **CROCK-POT**® slow cooker, here are guidelines for doubling or tripling ingredients:

- When preparing dishes with beef or pork in a larger unit, browning the meat in a skillet before adding to the **CROCK-POT**® slow cooker yields the best results; the meat will cook more evenly. Roasted meats, chicken, and turkey quantities may be doubled or tripled, and seasonings adjusted by half. Caution: Flavorful spices such as garlic and chili powder will intensify during long slow cooking. Add just 25 to 50 percent more spices as needed to balance the flavors.
- When preparing a soup or a stew, you may double all ingredients *except* liquids, seasonings and dried herbs. Increase liquid volume by half, or as needed. The **CROCK-POT**® slow cooker lid collects steam, which condenses to keep foods moist and maintain liquid volume. Do not double thickeners, such as cornstarch, at the beginning. You can always add more thickener later if needed.
- When preparing baked goods or cheesecakes, it is best to simply prepare the original recipe as many times as needed to serve more people.

Mexican

co

CINA

Easy Taco Dip

MAKES ABOUT 3 CUPS DIP

PREP TIME: 15 MINUTES
COOK TIME: 2 TO 4 HOURS (LOW) • 1 TO 2 HOURS (HIGH)

½ **pound ground beef chuck**
1 **cup frozen corn**
½ **cup chopped onion**
½ **cup salsa**
½ **cup mild taco sauce**
1 **can (4 ounces) diced mild green chilies**
1 **can (4 ounces) sliced ripe olives, drained**
1 **cup (4 ounces) shredded Mexican blend cheese**
   Tortilla chips
   Sour cream

1. Cook meat in large nonstick skillet over medium-high heat until no longer pink, stirring to separate; drain. Spoon into the **CROCK-POT**® slow cooker.

2. Add corn, onion, salsa, taco sauce, chilies and olives to slow cooker; stir to combine. Cover; cook on LOW for 2 to 4 hours or on HIGH for 1 to 2 hours.

3. Just before serving, stir in cheese. Serve with tortilla chips and sour cream.

Tip: To keep this dip hot for your entire party, simply leave it in the slow cooker on LOW or Warm setting.

South-of-the-Border Cumin Chicken

MAKES 4 SERVINGS

PREP TIME: 10 MINUTES
COOK TIME: 8 HOURS (LOW) • 4 HOURS (HIGH)

1 package (16 ounces) frozen bell pepper stir-fry mixture *or*
  3 bell peppers, sliced thin*
4 chicken drumsticks
4 chicken thighs
1 can (14½ ounces) stewed tomatoes
1 tablespoon mild pepper sauce
2 teaspoons sugar
1¾ teaspoons ground cumin, divided
1¼ teaspoons salt
1 teaspoon dried oregano leaves
¼ cup chopped fresh cilantro leaves
1 to 2 medium limes, cut in wedges

*If using fresh bell peppers, add 1 small onion, chopped.

1. Place bell pepper mixture in the **CROCK-POT**® slow cooker; place chicken on top.

2. Combine stewed tomatoes, pepper sauce, sugar, 1 teaspoon cumin, salt and oregano in large bowl. Pour over chicken mixture. Cover; cook on LOW for 8 hours or on HIGH for 4 hours or until meat is just beginning to fall off bones.

3. Place chicken in shallow serving bowl. Stir remaining ¾ teaspoon cumin into tomato mixture and pour over chicken. Sprinkle with cilantro; serve with lime wedges. Serve over cooked rice or with toasted corn tortillas, if desired.

South-of-the-Border Cumin Chicken

Spicy Tex-Mex Bowl

MAKES 8 TO 10 SERVINGS

PREP TIME: 35 MINUTES
COOK TIME: 5 TO 6 HOURS (LOW) • 3 TO 4 HOURS (HIGH)

⅓ **cup lentils**
1⅓ **cups water**
5 **strips bacon**
1 **onion, chopped**
1 **can (16 ounces) pinto beans, undrained**
1 **can (16 ounces) red kidney beans, undrained**
1 **can (15 ounces) diced tomatoes, undrained**
3 **tablespoons ketchup**
3 **cloves garlic, minced**
1 **teaspoon chili powder**
½ **teaspoon ground cumin**
¼ **teaspoon red pepper flakes**
1 **bay leaf**

1. Boil lentils in water 20 to 30 minutes in large saucepan; drain.

2. In small skillet, cook bacon until crisp; remove, drain and crumble bacon. In same skillet, cook onion in bacon drippings until soft.

3. Combine lentils, bacon, onion, beans with juice, tomatoes with juice, ketchup, garlic, chili powder, cumin, pepper flakes and bay leaf in the **CROCK-POT®** slow cooker. Cook on LOW for 5 to 6 hours or on HIGH for 3 to 4 hours. Remove bay leaf before serving.

Spicy Tex-Mex Bowl

Chicken Enchilada Roll-Ups

MAKES 6 SERVINGS

PREP TIME: 20 MINUTES
COOK TIME: 7 TO 8 HOURS (LOW) • 3 TO 4 HOURS (HIGH)

1½ **pounds boneless skinless chicken breasts**
½ **cup plus 2 tablespoons all-purpose flour, divided**
½ **teaspoon salt**
2 **tablespoons butter**
1 **cup chicken broth**
1 **small onion, diced**
¼ **to** ½ **cup canned jalapeño peppers, sliced**
½ **teaspoon dried oregano leaves**
2 **tablespoons cream or milk**
6 **flour tortillas (7 to 8 inches)**
6 **thin slices American cheese or American cheese with jalapeño peppers**

1. Cut each chicken breast lengthwise into 2 or 3 strips. Combine ½ cup flour and salt in plastic food storage bag. Add chicken strips and shake to coat with flour mixture. Melt butter in large skillet over medium heat. Brown chicken strips in batches 2 to 3 minutes per side. Place chicken into the **CROCK-POT®** slow cooker.

2. Add chicken broth to skillet and scrape up any browned bits. Pour broth mixture into slow cooker. Add onion, jalapeño peppers and oregano. Cover; cook on LOW for 7 to 8 hours or on HIGH for 3 to 4 hours or until chicken is tender and no longer pink in center.

3. Combine remaining 2 tablespoons flour and cream in small bowl; stir to form paste. Stir into chicken mixture; cook on HIGH until thickened.

4. Spoon chicken mixture onto center of flour tortillas. Top with 1 cheese slice. Roll up tortillas and serve.

Tip: This rich creamy chicken mixture can also be served over cooked rice.

Chicken Enchilada Roll-Up

Black Bean-Stuffed Peppers

MAKES 6 SERVINGS

PREP TIME: 15 MINUTES
COOK TIME: 6 TO 8 HOURS (LOW) • 3 TO 4 HOURS (HIGH)

1 medium onion, finely chopped
    Nonstick cooking spray
¼ teaspoon cayenne pepper
¼ teaspoon dried oregano
¼ teaspoon ground cumin
¼ teaspoon chili powder
1 can (15 ounces) black beans, rinsed and drained, divided
6 tall green bell peppers, tops removed, seeded and cored
1 cup (4 ounces) shredded reduced-fat Monterey Jack cheese
1 cup tomato salsa
½ cup fat-free sour cream

1. Cook the onion in a medium skillet, sprayed with cooking spray, until golden. Add the cayenne pepper, oregano, cumin and chili powder.

2. Mash half the black beans with the cooked onion in a medium mixing bowl. Stir in the remaining beans. Place the bell peppers in the **CROCK-POT®** slow cooker; spoon the black bean mixture into the bell peppers. Sprinkle the cheese over the peppers. Pour the salsa over the cheese. Cover; cook on LOW for 6 to 8 hours or on HIGH for 3 to 4 hours.

3. Serve each pepper with a dollop of sour cream.

Black Bean-Stuffed Pepper

Mexicali Chicken

MAKES 4 SERVINGS

PREP TIME: 10 MINUTES
COOK TIME: 7 TO 8 HOURS (LOW) • 2 TO 3 HOURS (HIGH)

2 medium green bell peppers, cut into thin strips
1 large onion, quartered and thinly sliced
4 chicken thighs
4 chicken drumsticks
1 tablespoon chili powder
2 teaspoons dried oregano leaves
1 jar (16 ounces) chipotle salsa
½ cup ketchup
2 teaspoons ground cumin
½ teaspoon salt
   Hot cooked noodles

1. Place bell peppers and onion in the **CROCK-POT®** slow cooker; top with chicken. Sprinkle chili powder and oregano evenly over chicken. Add salsa. Cover; cook on LOW for 7 to 8 hours or on HIGH for 2 to 3 hours or until chicken is tender.

2. Remove chicken pieces to serving bowl; keep warm. Stir ketchup, cumin and salt into liquid in slow cooker. Cook, uncovered, on HIGH 15 minutes or until hot.

3. Pour mixture over chicken. Serve with noodles.

Tip: For thicker sauce, blend 1 tablespoon cornstarch and 2 tablespoons water. Stir into cooking liquid with ketchup, cumin and salt.

Campbell's® Mexican Beef & Bean Stew

MAKES 6 SERVINGS

PREP TIME: 10 MINUTES
COOK TIME: 8 TO 10 HOURS (LOW) • 4 TO 5 HOURS (HIGH)

1½ **pounds beef for stew, cut into 1-inch cubes**
  2 tablespoons all-purpose flour
  1 tablespoon vegetable oil
  1 cup coarsely chopped onion
  1 can (about 15 ounces) pinto beans, drained
  1 can (about 16 ounces) whole kernel corn, drained
  1 can CAMPBELL'S® Condensed Beef Consommé
  1 cup PACE® Chunky Salsa
  2 tablespoons chili powder
  1 teaspoon ground cumin
 ¼ **teaspoon garlic powder *or* 2 cloves garlic, minced**

1. Coat beef with flour. Heat oil in skillet. Add beef and cook until browned.

2. Place beef, onion, beans, corn, consommé, salsa, chili powder, cumin and garlic powder in the **CROCK-POT®** slow cooker.

3. Cover and cook on LOW for 8 to 10 hours or on HIGH for 4 to 5 hours or until done.

Campbell's Is Cooking With Rival®!

Opening the lid and checking on food in the slow cooker can affect both cooking time and results. Due to the nature of slow cooking, there is no need to stir the food unless the recipe method says to do so.

Three-Bean Mole Chili

MAKES 4 TO 6 SERVINGS

PREP TIME: 10 MINUTES
COOK TIME: 5 TO 6 HOURS (LOW) • 1 TO 2 HOURS (HIGH)

1 can (15 ounces) pinto beans, rinsed and drained
1 can (15 ounces) chili beans in spicy sauce, undrained
1 can (15 ounces) black beans, rinsed and drained
1 can (14½ ounces) Mexican or chili-style diced tomatoes, undrained
1 large green bell pepper, diced
1 small onion, diced
½ cup beef, chicken or vegetable broth
¼ cup prepared mole paste*
2 teaspoons ground cumin
2 teaspoons ground coriander (optional)
2 teaspoons chili powder
2 teaspoons minced garlic
Toppings: crushed tortilla chips, chopped cilantro or shredded cheese (optional)

*Mole paste is available in the Mexican section of large supermarkets or in specialty markets.

1. Combine beans, tomatoes with juice, bell pepper, onion, broth, mole paste, cumin, coriander, if desired, chili powder and garlic in the **CROCK-POT®** slow cooker; mix well.

2. Cover; cook on LOW for 5 to 6 hours or on HIGH for 1 to 2 hours or until vegetables are tender.

3. Serve with toppings, if desired.

Three-Bean Mole Chili

Italian **CU**

CINA

Italian-Style Sausage with Rice

MAKES 4 TO 5 SERVINGS

PREP TIME: 10 TO 15 MINUTES
COOK TIME: 4 TO 6 HOURS (LOW) • 2 TO 3 HOURS (HIGH)

1 **pound mild Italian sausage, cut into 1-inch pieces**
1 **can (29 ounces) pinto beans, rinsed and drained**
1 **cup spaghetti sauce**
1 **green bell pepper, cut into strips**
1 **small onion, halved and sliced**
½ **teaspoon salt**
¼ **teaspoon black pepper**
  Hot cooked rice
  Chopped fresh basil (optional)

1. Brown sausage in large nonstick skillet over medium heat. Pour off drippings.

2. Place sausage, beans, spaghetti sauce, bell pepper, onion, salt and pepper into the **CROCK-POT®** slow cooker. Cover; cook on LOW for 4 to 6 hours or on HIGH for 2 to 3 hours.

3. Serve with rice. Garnish with basil, if desired.

Tarragon Turkey & Pasta

MAKES 4 SERVINGS

PREP TIME: 15 TO 20 MINUTES
COOK TIME: 6 TO 8 HOURS (LOW) • 3½ TO 4 HOURS (HIGH)

1½ **to 2 pounds turkey tenderloins**
½ **cup thinly sliced celery**
¼ **cup thinly sliced green onions**
4 **tablespoons minced fresh tarragon, divided**
¼ **cup dry white wine**
1 **teaspoon salt**
1 **teaspoon black pepper**
½ **cup plain yogurt**
2 **tablespoons minced fresh Italian parsley**
2 **tablespoons lemon juice**
1½ **tablespoons cornstarch**
2 **tablespoons water**
4 **cups pasta of your choice, cooked al denté**

1. Combine the turkey, celery, green onions, 2 tablespoons fresh tarragon, wine, salt and pepper in the **CROCK-POT**® slow cooker. Mix thoroughly. Cover; cook on LOW for 6 to 8 hours or on HIGH for 3½ to 4 hours or until turkey is no longer pink.

2. Remove the turkey from the stoneware and cut it into ½-inch-thick medallions. Turn the **CROCK-POT**® slow cooker to HIGH. Add the yogurt, remaining 2 tablespoons fresh tarragon, parsley and lemon juice to the juices in the stoneware.

3. In a small bowl, combine the cornstarch and water. Add the mixture to the stoneware and cook until the juices thicken. Serve the turkey medallions over the pasta with the tarragon sauce.

Tarragon Turkey & Pasta

Herbed Artichoke Chicken

MAKES 6 SERVINGS

PREP TIME: 5 MINUTES
COOK TIME: 6 TO 8 HOURS (LOW) • 3½ TO 4 HOURS (HIGH)

1½ pounds skinless, boneless chicken breasts
1 can (14 ounces) tomatoes, drained and diced
1 can (14 ounces) artichoke hearts in water, drained
1 small onion, chopped
½ cup kalamata olives, pitted and sliced
1 cup nonfat chicken broth
¼ cup dry white wine
3 tablespoons quick-cooking tapioca
2 teaspoons curry powder
1 tablespoon fresh Italian parsley sprigs, chopped
1 teaspoon dried basil leaves
1 teaspoon dried thyme leaves
½ teaspoon salt
½ teaspoon freshly ground black pepper

1. Combine chicken, tomatoes, artichokes, onion, olives, broth, wine, tapioca, curry powder, parsley, basil, thyme, salt and pepper in the **CROCK-POT**® slow cooker. Mix thoroughly.

2. Cover; cook on LOW for 6 to 8 hours or on HIGH for 3½ to 4 hours or until chicken is no longer pink in center.

Herbed Artichoke Chicken

Three Pepper Pasta Sauce

MAKES 4 TO 6 SERVINGS

PREP TIME: 10 TO 15 MINUTES
COOK TIME: 7 TO 8 HOURS (LOW) ● 3 TO 4 HOURS (HIGH)

1 red bell pepper, cut into 1-inch pieces
1 green bell pepper, cut into 1-inch pieces
1 yellow bell pepper, cut into 1-inch pieces
2 cans (14½ ounces each) diced tomatoes, undrained
1 cup chopped onion
1 can (6 ounces) tomato paste
4 cloves garlic, minced
2 tablespoons olive oil
1 teaspoon dried basil leaves
1 teaspoon dried oregano leaves
½ teaspoon salt
¼ teaspoon red pepper flakes or ground black pepper
  Hot cooked pasta of your choice
  Grated Parmesan or Romano cheese

1. Combine all ingredients except pasta and cheese in the **CROCK-POT**® slow cooker. Cover; cook on LOW for 7 to 8 hours or on HIGH for 3 to 4 hours or until vegetables are tender.

2. Adjust seasonings, if desired. Serve with pasta and cheese.

Tip: You can substitute 3 cups mixed bell pepper chunks from a salad bar for the peppers.

Three Pepper Pasta Sauce

Eggplant Italiano

MAKES 6 SERVINGS

PREP TIME: 10 MINUTES
COOK TIME: 4 TO 5 HOURS (LOW)

1¼ **pounds eggplant, cut into 1-inch cubes**
2 **medium onions, thinly sliced**
2 **ribs celery, cut into 1-inch pieces**
1 **can (16 ounces) diced tomatoes, undrained**
3 **tablespoons tomato sauce**
1 **tablespoon olive oil**
½ **cup pitted ripe olives, cut in half**
2 **tablespoons balsamic vinegar**
1 **tablespoon sugar**
1 **tablespoon drained capers**
1 **teaspoon dried oregano or basil leaves**
Salt and black pepper
Fresh basil leaves, leaf lettuce and red jalapeño pepper* (optional)

*Jalapeño peppers can sting and irritate the skin; wear rubber gloves when handling peppers and do not touch eyes. Wash hands after handling.

1. Combine eggplant, onions, celery, tomatoes with juice, tomato sauce and oil in the **CROCK-POT**® slow cooker.

2. Cover; cook on LOW for 3½ to 4 hours or until eggplant is tender.

3. Stir in olives, vinegar, sugar, capers and oregano. Season to taste with salt and pepper. Cover and cook 45 minutes to 1 hour or until heated through. Garnish, if desired.

Campbell's® Zesty Italian Pot Roast

MAKES 4 TO 6 SERVINGS

PREP TIME: 10 MINUTES
COOK TIME: 10 TO 12 HOURS (LOW) • 4 TO 6 HOURS (HIGH)

4 medium potatoes, quartered (about 4 cups)
2 cups fresh or frozen baby carrots
1 stalk celery, cut into 1-inch pieces
½ cup diced plum tomato
1 (2½-pound) boneless beef chuck roast
½ teaspoon black pepper
1 can (10¾ ounces) CAMPBELL'S® Tomato Soup
½ cup water
1 tablespoon roasted garlic*
1 teaspoon dried basil
1 teaspoon dried oregano
1 teaspoon dried parsley flakes, crushed
1 teaspoon vinegar

*To roast garlic, place whole garlic bulb on piece of aluminum foil. Drizzle with a little oil and wrap. Roast in oven at 350°F for 45 minutes or until soft.

1. Place potatoes, carrots, celery and tomato in the **CROCK-POT®** slow cooker. Season roast with pepper and place on top of vegetables.

2. Mix together soup, water, garlic, basil, oregano, parsley and vinegar. Pour over meat and vegetables in stoneware.

3. Cover and cook on LOW for 10 to 12 hours or on HIGH for 4 to 6 hours or until done.

Campbell's Is Cooking With Rival®!

For thicker gravy, mix ¼ cup all-purpose flour with ½ cup water. Remove beef from stoneware. Add flour mixture to stoneware. Turn heat to HIGH. Cook until mixture thickens, about 10 minutes.

Winter
WA

RMERS

Chicken and Sweet Potato Stew

MAKES 6 SERVINGS

PREP TIME: 15 MINUTES
COOK TIME: 6 TO 8 HOURS (LOW) ● 3 TO 4 HOURS (HIGH)

4 boneless, skinless chicken breasts, cut into bite-size pieces
2 medium sweet potatoes, peeled and cubed
2 medium Yukon Gold potatoes, peeled and cubed
2 medium carrots, peeled and cut into ½-inch slices
1 can (28 ounces) whole stewed tomatoes
1 teaspoon salt
1 teaspoon paprika
1 teaspoon celery seed
½ teaspoon freshly ground black pepper
⅛ teaspoon ground cinnamon
⅛ teaspoon ground nutmeg
1 cup nonfat, low-sodium chicken broth
¼ cup fresh basil leaves, chopped

1. Combine chicken, potatoes, carrots, tomatoes, salt, paprika, celery seed, pepper, cinnamon, nutmeg and broth in the **CROCK-POT®** slow cooker.

2. Cover; cook on LOW for 6 to 8 hours or on HIGH for 3 to 4 hours.

3. Sprinkle with basil just before serving.

Note: This light stew has an Indian influence and offers excellent flavor without the fat.

Italian Beef and Barley Soup

MAKES 6 SERVINGS

PREP TIME: 20 MINUTES
COOK TIME: 8 TO 10 HOURS (LOW) ● 3 TO 4 HOURS (HIGH)

1 boneless beef top sirloin steak (about 1½ pounds)
1 tablespoon vegetable oil
4 medium carrots or parsnips, sliced ¼ inch thick
1 cup chopped onion
1 teaspoon dried thyme leaves
½ teaspoon dried rosemary
¼ teaspoon black pepper
⅓ cup pearl barley
2 cans (14½ ounces each) beef broth
1 can (14½ ounces) diced tomatoes with Italian seasoning, undrained

1. Cut beef into 1-inch pieces. Heat oil over medium-high heat in large skillet; brown beef on all sides. Set aside.

2. Place carrots and onion in the **CROCK-POT**® slow cooker; sprinkle with thyme, rosemary and pepper. Top with barley and meat. Pour broth and tomatoes with juice over meat. Cover; cook on LOW for 8 to 10 hours or on HIGH for 3 to 4 hours or until beef is tender.

Italian Beef and Barley Soup

Parsnip and Carrot Soup

MAKES 4 SERVING

PREP TIME: 15 MINUTES
COOK TIME: 6 TO 9 HOURS (LOW) • 2 TO 4 HOURS (HIGH)

1 medium leek, thinly sliced
  Nonstick cooking spray
4 medium parsnips, peeled and diced
4 medium carrots, peeled and diced
4 cups nonfat chicken broth or stock
1 bay leaf
½ teaspoon salt
½ teaspoon freshly ground pepper
½ cup small pasta, cooked al denté and drained
1 tablespoon Italian parsley sprigs, chopped
1 cup low-fat croutons

1. Cook the leek in a small nonstick skillet, sprayed with cooking spray, over medium heat until golden. Place in the **CROCK-POT**® slow cooker.

2. Add the parsnips, carrots, broth, bay leaf, salt and pepper. Cover; cook on LOW for 6 to 9 hours or on HIGH for 2 to 4 hours or until the vegetables are tender.

3. Add the pasta during the last hour of cooking. Remove bay leaf. Sprinkle each individual serving with parsley and croutons.

Note: This dish is a great year-round accompaniment to a main course of roasted meat. Or, the soup can stand alone as a quick, satisfying meal.

Parsnip and Carrot Soup

Wild Mushroom Beef Stew

MAKES 5 SERVINGS

PREP TIME: 15 TO 20 MINUTES
COOK TIME: 10 TO 12 HOURS (LOW) • 4 TO 6 HOURS (HIGH)

1½ to 2 pounds beef stew meat, cut into 1-inch cubes
  2 tablespoons all-purpose flour
  ½ teaspoon salt
  ½ teaspoon black pepper
1½ cups beef broth
  1 teaspoon Worcestershire sauce
  1 clove garlic, minced
  1 bay leaf
  1 teaspoon paprika
  4 shiitake mushrooms, sliced
  2 medium carrots, sliced
  2 medium potatoes, diced
  1 small white onion, chopped
  1 stalk celery, sliced

1. Put the beef in the **CROCK-POT**® slow cooker. Mix together the flour, salt and pepper and sprinkle over the meat; stir to coat each piece of meat with flour. Add the remaining ingredients and stir to mix well.

2. Cover; cook on LOW for 10 to 12 hours or on HIGH for 4 to 6 hours. Stir the stew before serving.

Note: If shiitake mushrooms are unavailable in your local grocery store, you can substitute other mushrooms of your choice. For an extra punch of flavor, add a few dried porcini mushrooms to the stew.

Wild Mushroom Beef Stew

Chicken Provençal

MAKES 8 SERVINGS

PREP TIME: 15 TO 20 MINUTES
COOK TIME: 7 TO 9 HOURS (LOW) • 3 TO 4 HOURS (HIGH)

2 pounds boneless, skinless chicken thighs, each cut into quarters
2 medium red bell peppers, cut into ¼-inch-thick slices
1 medium yellow bell pepper, cut into ¼-inch-thick slices
1 onion, thinly sliced
1 (28-ounce) can plum tomatoes, drained
3 cloves garlic, minced
¼ teaspoon salt
¼ teaspoon thyme
¼ teaspoon fennel seeds, crushed
3 strips orange peel
½ cup fresh basil leaves, chopped

1. Place thighs, bell peppers, onion, tomatoes, garlic, salt, thyme, fennel seeds and orange peel in the **CROCK-POT®** slow cooker. Mix thoroughly.

2. Cover; cook on LOW for 7 to 9 hours or on HIGH for 3 to 4 hours.

3. Sprinkle with basil and serve.

Serving Suggestion: Serve with a crusty French baguette and seasonal vegetables.

Chicken Provençal

Winter's Best Bean Soup

MAKES 8 TO 10 SERVINGS

PREP TIME: 15 MINUTES
COOK TIME: 8 HOURS (LOW) • 4 HOURS (HIGH)

6 ounces bacon, diced
10 cups chicken broth
3 cans (15 ounces each) Great Northern beans, rinsed and drained
1 can (14½ ounces) diced tomatoes, undrained
1 package (10 ounces) frozen sliced or diced carrots
1 large onion, chopped
2 teaspoons bottled minced garlic
1 fresh rosemary sprig or 1 teaspoon dried rosemary
1 teaspoon ground black pepper

1. Cook bacon in medium skillet over medium-high heat until crisp; drain and place in the **CROCK-POT®** slow cooker.

2. Add broth, beans, tomatoes with juice, carrots, onion, garlic, rosemary and pepper.

3. Cover; cook on LOW for 8 hours or on HIGH for 4 hours or until beans are tender. Remove rosemary sprig and mince the leaves. Return to soup; mix well before serving.

Serving Suggestion: Place slices of toasted Italian bread in bottom of individual soup bowls. Drizzle with olive oil. Pour soup over bread and serve.

Winter's Best Bean Soup

Asian
FLA

VORS

Spicy Asian Pork Filling

MAKES 20 (¼-CUP) SERVINGS

PREP TIME: 15 TO 20 MINUTES
COOK TIME: 8 TO 10 HOURS (LOW) ● 4 TO 5 HOURS (HIGH)

1 (3-pound) boneless pork sirloin roast, cut into 2- to 3-inch chunks
½ cup tamari sauce or soy sauce
1 tablespoon chili garlic sauce or chili paste
2 teaspoons minced fresh ginger
2 tablespoons water
1 tablespoon cornstarch
2 teaspoons dark sesame oil

1. Combine pork, tamari sauce, chili garlic sauce and ginger in the **CROCK-POT**® slow cooker; mix well. Cover; cook on LOW for 8 to 10 hours or on HIGH for 4 to 5 hours or until pork is fork tender.

2. Remove roast from cooking liquid; cool slightly. Trim and discard excess fat. Shred the pork using 2 forks. Let liquid stand 5 minutes to allow fat to rise. Skim off fat.

3. Combine water, cornstarch and sesame oil until smooth; whisk into pan juices. Cook on HIGH until thickened. Add shredded meat to stoneware; mix well. Cook 15 to 30 minutes or until hot.

Spicy Asian Pork Bundles: Place ¼ cup pork filling into large lettuce leaves. Wrap to enclose. Makes about 20 bundles.

Moo Shu Pork: Lightly spread plum sauce over warm small flour tortillas. Spoon ¼ cup pork filling and ¼ cup stir-fried vegetables into flour tortillas. Wrap to enclose. Serve immediately. Makes enough to fill about 20 tortillas.

Slow-Simmered Curried Chicken

MAKES 4 SERVINGS

PREP TIME: 15 TO 20 MINUTES
COOK TIME: 5 TO 6 HOURS (LOW) • 2 TO 3 HOURS (HIGH)

1½ **cups chopped onions**
  1 **medium green bell pepper, chopped**
  1 **pound boneless skinless chicken breasts or thighs, cut into bite-size pieces**
  1 **cup medium salsa**
  2 **teaspoons grated fresh ginger**
  ½ **teaspoon garlic powder**
  ½ **teaspoon red pepper flakes**
  ¼ **cup chopped fresh cilantro**
  1 **teaspoon sugar**
  1 **teaspoon curry powder**
  ¾ **teaspoon salt**
    Hot cooked rice

1. Place onions and bell pepper in the **CROCK-POT**® slow cooker. Top with chicken. Combine salsa, ginger, garlic powder and pepper flakes in small bowl; spoon over chicken. Cover; cook on LOW for 5 to 6 hours or on HIGH for 2 to 3 hours or until chicken is tender.

2. Combine cilantro, sugar, curry powder and salt in small bowl. Stir mixture into stoneware. Cover; cook on HIGH 15 minutes or until hot.

3. Serve with rice.

Slow-Simmered Curried Chicken

Simmering Hot & Sour Soup

MAKES 4 SERVINGS

PREP TIME: 10 TO 15 MINUTES
COOK TIME: 3 TO 4 HOURS (LOW) • 2 TO 3 HOURS (HIGH)

2 cans (about 14 ounces each) chicken broth
1 cup chopped cooked chicken or pork
4 ounces fresh shiitake mushroom caps, thinly sliced
½ cup sliced bamboo shoots, cut into thin strips
3 tablespoons rice vinegar or rice wine vinegar
2 tablespoons soy sauce
1½ teaspoons chili paste *or* 1 teaspoon hot chili oil
4 ounces firm tofu, well drained and cut into ½-inch pieces
2 teaspoons dark sesame oil
2 tablespoons cornstarch
2 tablespoons cold water
    Chopped cilantro or sliced green onions

1. Combine chicken broth, chicken, mushrooms, bamboo shoots, vinegar, soy sauce and chili paste in the **CROCK-POT®** slow cooker. Cover; cook on LOW for 3 to 4 hours or on HIGH for 2 to 3 hours.

2. Stir in tofu and sesame oil. Combine cornstarch with water; mix well. Stir into stoneware. Cover; cook on HIGH 10 minutes or until soup is thickened.

3. Garnish with cilantro and green onions.

Simmering Hot & Sour Soup

Sweet and Sour Shrimp

MAKES 4 TO 6 SERVINGS

PREP TIME: 15 TO 20 MINUTES
COOK TIME: 3 TO 4 HOURS (LOW) • 2 TO 3 HOURS (HIGH)

1 can (16 ounces) sliced peaches in syrup, undrained
½ cup chopped green onions
½ cup chopped red bell pepper
½ cup chopped green bell pepper
½ cup chopped celery
⅓ cup vegetable broth
2 tablespoons dark sesame oil
¼ cup light soy sauce
2 tablespoons rice wine vinegar
1 teaspoon red pepper flakes
6 ounces snow peas
1 pound cooked medium shrimp
1 cup cherry tomatoes, cut into halves
½ cup toasted walnut pieces

1. Place peaches, onions, peppers, celery, broth, sesame oil, soy sauce, vinegar and pepper flakes in the **CROCK-POT®** slow cooker. Cover; cook on LOW for 3 to 4 hours or on HIGH for 2 to 3 hours or until vegetables are tender. Stir well.

2. Add snow peas. Cook 15 minutes on HIGH. Add shrimp, tomatoes and walnuts. Cook 4 to 5 minutes on HIGH or until shrimp is hot.

3. Serve with rice.

Sweet and Sour Shrimp

Asian-Spiced Chicken Wings

MAKES 10 TO 16 WINGS

PREP TIME: 20 TO 25 MINUTES
COOK TIME: 5 TO 6 HOURS (LOW) • 2 TO 3 HOURS (HIGH)

  3 **pounds chicken wings**
  1 **cup packed brown sugar**
  1 **cup soy sauce**
½ **cup ketchup**
  1 **teaspoon minced fresh ginger**
  1 **clove garlic, minced**
¼ **cup dry sherry**
½ **cup hoisin sauce**
  1 **tablespoon fresh lime juice**
  3 **tablespoons sesame seeds, toasted**
¼ **cup thinly sliced green onions**

1. Broil the chicken wings 10 minutes on each side or until browned. Transfer the chicken wings to the **CROCK-POT®** slow cooker. Add the brown sugar, soy sauce, ketchup, ginger, garlic and sherry; stir thoroughly. Cover; cook on LOW for 5 to 6 hours or on HIGH for 2 to 3 hours or until the wings are no longer pink, stirring once halfway through the cooking time to baste the wings with sauce.

2. Remove the wings from the stoneware. Reserve ¼ cup of the remaining juices; combine with the hoisin sauce and lime juice. Drizzle mixture over the wings.

3. Before serving, sprinkle the wings with the sesame seeds and green onions.

Note: Chicken wings are always crowd pleasers. Garnishing them with toasted sesame seeds and green onions gives these appetizers added crunch and contrasting color.

Asian-Spiced Chicken Wings

 **ASIAN FLAVORS**

Korean BBQ Beef Short Ribs

MAKES 6 SERVINGS

PREP TIME: 10 TO 15 MINUTES
COOK TIME: 7 TO 8 HOURS (LOW) • 3 TO 4 HOURS (HIGH)

4 to 4½ pounds beef short ribs
¼ cup chopped green onions with tops
¼ cup tamari sauce or soy sauce
¼ cup beef broth or water
1 tablespoon brown sugar
2 teaspoons minced fresh ginger
2 teaspoons minced garlic
½ teaspoon black pepper
2 teaspoons dark sesame oil
   Hot cooked rice or linguini pasta
2 teaspoons sesame seeds, toasted

1. Place ribs in the **CROCK-POT®** slow cooker. Combine green onions, tamari, broth, brown sugar, ginger, garlic and pepper in medium bowl; mix well and pour over ribs. Cover; cook on LOW for 7 to 8 hours or on HIGH for 3 to 4 hours or until ribs are fork tender.

2. Remove ribs from cooking liquid; cool slightly. Trim excess fat from ribs. Cut rib meat into bite-size pieces discarding bones and fat.

3. Let cooking liquid stand 5 minutes to allow fat to rise. Skim off fat.

4. Stir sesame oil into liquid. Return beef to slow cooker. Cover; cook on LOW for 15 to 30 minutes or until mixture is hot.

5. Serve with rice; garnish with sesame seeds.

Variation: Three pounds boneless short ribs can be substituted for beef short ribs.

Korean BBQ Beef Short Ribs

Casual
CHIL
BBQ

Campbell's® Hearty Beef & Bean Chili

MAKES 6 SERVINGS

PREP TIME: 10 MINUTES
COOK TIME: 8 TO 10 HOURS (LOW) • 4 TO 5 HOURS (HIGH)

1½ **pounds ground beef**
1 **large onion, chopped**
2 **cloves garlic, minced**
1 **can (10¾ ounces) CAMPBELL'S® Tomato Soup**
1 **can (14½ ounces) diced tomatoes**
½ **cup water**
2 **cans (about 15 ounces each) red kidney beans**
¼ **cup chili powder**
2 **teaspoons ground cumin**

1. Cook beef in skillet until browned. Pour off fat.

2. Mix beef, onion, garlic, soup, tomatoes, water, beans, chili powder and cumin in the **CROCK-POT®** slow cooker.

3. Cover and cook on LOW for 8 to 10 hours or on HIGH for 4 to 5 hours or until done.

Fiery Chili Beef

MAKES 6 SERVINGS

PREP TIME: 15 MINUTES
COOK TIME: 7 TO 8 HOURS (LOW) ● 3 TO 4 HOURS (HIGH)

1 (1- to 1½-pound) beef flank steak
1 can (28 ounces) diced tomatoes, undrained
1 can (15 ounces) pinto beans, rinsed and drained
1 medium onion, chopped
2 cloves garlic, minced
½ teaspoon salt
½ teaspoon ground cumin
¼ teaspoon black pepper
1 canned chipotle chile pepper in adobo sauce
1 teaspoon adobo sauce from canned chile pepper
Flour tortillas

1. Cut flank steak into 6 equal pieces. Place flank steak, tomatoes with juice, beans, onion, garlic, salt, cumin and black pepper into the **CROCK-POT**® slow cooker.

2. Dice chile pepper. Add pepper and adobo sauce to stoneware; mix well. Cover; cook on LOW for 7 to 8 hours or on HIGH for 3 to 4 hours or until steak is tender. Serve with tortillas.

Crock-Pot® Stoneware Slow Cooker *Tip*

Chipotle chile peppers are dried, smoked jalapeño peppers with a very hot yet smoky, sweet flavor. They can be found dried, pickled, and canned in adobo sauce.

Fiery Chili Beef

Bean and Corn Chili

MAKES 6 SERVINGS

PREP TIME: 15 TO 20 MINUTES
COOK TIME: 6 TO 8 HOURS (LOW) • 3 TO 4 HOURS (HIGH)

2 medium onions, finely chopped
5 cloves garlic, minced
½ teaspoon olive oil
2 tablespoons red wine
1 green bell pepper, seeded and finely chopped
1 red bell pepper, seeded and finely chopped
1 stalk celery, finely sliced
6 Roma tomatoes, chopped
2 cans (15 ounces each) kidney beans, rinsed and drained
1 can (6 ounces) tomato paste
1 cup frozen corn kernels
1 teaspoon salt
1 teaspoon chili powder
½ teaspoon black pepper
¼ teaspoon cumin
¼ teaspoon cayenne pepper
¼ teaspoon dried oregano leaves
¼ teaspoon ground coriander
1½ cups nonfat chicken or vegetable broth

1. Cook the onions and garlic in the olive oil and red wine in a medium skillet until onions are tender. Add the onion mixture and the bell peppers, celery, tomatoes, beans, tomato paste, corn, salt, chili powder, black pepper, cumin, cayenne pepper, oregano, coriander and broth to the **CROCK-POT®** slow cooker. Mix thoroughly.

2. Cover; cook on LOW for 6 to 8 hours or on HIGH for 3 to 4 hours.

Bean and Corn Chili

Barbecued Beef Sandwiches

MAKES 12 SERVINGS

PREP TIME: 20 TO 25 MINUTES
COOK TIME: 8 TO 10 HOURS (LOW) • 4 TO 5 HOURS (HIGH)

3 pounds boneless beef chuck shoulder roast
2 cups ketchup
1 medium onion, chopped
¼ cup cider vinegar
¼ cup dark molasses
2 tablespoons Worcestershire sauce
2 cloves garlic, minced
½ teaspoon salt
½ teaspoon dry mustard
½ teaspoon black pepper
¼ teaspoon garlic powder
¼ teaspoon red pepper flakes
    Sesame seed buns, split

1. Cut roast in half and place into the **CROCK-POT®** slow cooker. Combine remaining ingredients except buns in large bowl. Pour sauce mixture over roast. Cover; cook on LOW for 8 to 10 hours or on HIGH for 4 to 5 hours or until roast is tender.

2. Remove roast from cooking liquid; cool slightly. Trim and discard excess fat from beef. Using 2 forks, shred meat.

3. Let cooking liquid stand 5 minutes to allow fat to rise. Skim off fat.

4. Return shredded meat to slow cooker. Stir meat to evenly coat with sauce. Adjust seasonings, if desired. Cover; cook on LOW for 15 to 30 minutes or until meat is hot.

5. Spoon filling into buns and top with additional barbecue sauce, if desired.

Barbecued Beef Sandwich

McCormick® Weeknight Chili

MAKES 4 SERVINGS

PREP TIME: 5 MINUTES
COOK TIME: 1 TO 2 HOURS (LOW) • 1 HOUR (HIGH)

1 pound ground beef or ground turkey
2 cans (8 ounces each) tomato sauce
1 can (15 ounces) red kidney beans, undrained
1 package (1¼ ounces) McCormick® Chili Seasoning
1 cup shredded Cheddar cheese
Chopped onion (optional)

1. Cook ground beef or turkey in a 12-inch skillet until no longer pink, stirring often; drain.

2. Scrape contents of skillet into the **CROCK-POT®** slow cooker. Stir in tomato sauce, beans and seasoning. Cover and cook on LOW for 1 to 2 hours or on HIGH for 45 minutes to 1 hour, or until done.

3. Stir chili before serving. Top with cheese and onion if desired.

Is Cooking With Rival®!

For an American regional twist, try making this chili Cincinnati style! Just add 1 teaspoon **McCormick® Ground Cinnamon** and serve the chili over boiled macaroni elbow noodles.

McCormick® Weeknight Chili

Rio Grande Ribs

MAKES 6 SERVINGS

PREP TIME: 15 MINUTES
COOK TIME: 6 HOURS (LOW) • 3 HOURS (HIGH)

4 pounds country-style pork ribs, trimmed of all visible fat
Salt, to taste
Black pepper, to taste
1 jar (16 ounces) picante sauce
½ cup beer, nonalcoholic malt beverage or beef broth
¼ cup *Frank's® RedHot®* Cayenne Pepper Sauce
1 teaspoon chili powder
2 cups *French's®* French Fried Onions

1. Season ribs with salt and pepper. Broil ribs 6 inches from heat on rack in broiler pan for 10 minutes or until well-browned, turning once. Place ribs in the **CROCK-POT®** slow cooker. Combine picante sauce, beer, *Frank's® RedHot®* Cayenne Pepper Sauce and chili powder in small bowl. Pour mixture over top.

2. Cover and cook on LOW for 6 hours or on HIGH for 3 hours or until ribs are tender. Transfer ribs to serving platter; keep warm. Skim fat from liquid.

3. Turn the **CROCK-POT®** slow cooker to HIGH. Add 1 cup *French's® French Fried Onions* to the stoneware. Cook 10 to 15 minutes or until slightly thickened. Spoon sauce over ribs and sprinkle with remaining 1 cup *French Fried Onions*. Splash on more *Frank's® RedHot®* Cayenne Pepper Sauce to taste.

Tip: Prepare ingredients the night before for quick assembly in the morning. Keep refrigerated until ready to cook.

BUSH'S® BEST 3-Bean Chili

MAKES 8 SERVINGS

PREP TIME: 15 MINUTES
COOK TIME: 3 TO 4 HOURS (LOW) • 2 TO 3 HOURS (HIGH)

2 pounds lean ground round beef
3 teaspoons chili powder
1 small yellow onion, chopped
1 small green bell pepper, seeded and chopped
2 cans (16 ounces) BUSH'S® BEST Dark Red Kidney Beans
2 cans (16 ounces) BUSH'S® BEST Pinto Beans
2 cans (15 ounces) BUSH'S® BEST Black Beans
1 can (14½ ounces) diced tomatoes
1 can (6 ounces) tomato paste
1½ teaspoons salt
1 teaspoon garlic salt
½ teaspoon black pepper
½ teaspoon ground cumin
⅛ teaspoon ground cinnamon
Sour cream (optional)

1. Brown ground beef in large skillet. Drain excess fat and scrape contents of skillet into the **CROCK-POT**® slow cooker. Add chili powder, onion, green pepper, beans, tomatoes, tomato paste, salt, garlic salt, black pepper, cumin and cinnamon.

2. Cover and cook on LOW for 3 to 4 hours or on HIGH for 2 to 3 hours.

3. Garnish with sour cream, if desired.

American
CLA

SSICS

Barbecued Pulled Pork Sandwiches

MAKES 8 SERVINGS

PREP TIME: 15 TO 20 MINUTES
COOK TIME: 12 TO 14 HOURS (LOW) ● 6 TO 7 HOURS (HIGH)

1 (2½-pound) pork roast
1 bottle (14 ounces) of your favorite barbecue sauce
1 teaspoon brown sugar
1 tablespoon fresh lemon juice
1 medium onion, chopped
8 hamburger buns or hard rolls

1. Place the pork roast in the **CROCK-POT**® slow cooker. Cover; cook on LOW for 10 to 12 hours or on HIGH for 5 to 6 hours or until pork roast is tender.

2. Remove the pork roast from the stoneware. Shred the pork with 2 forks. Pour out any liquid in the stoneware. Return the pork to the stoneware; add the barbecue sauce, brown sugar, lemon juice and onion. Cook on HIGH for 1 hour or on LOW for 2 hours.

3. Serve the pork on hamburger buns or hard rolls.

Note: This kid-popular dish is sweet and savory, and most importantly, extremely easy to make. Serve with crunchy coleslaw on the side.

Spinach Gorgonzola Corn Bread

MAKES 10 TO 12 SERVINGS

PREP TIME: 8 MINUTES
COOK TIME: 1½ HOURS (HIGH)

2 boxes (8½ ounces each) corn bread mix
3 eggs
½ cup cream
1 box (10 ounces) frozen chopped spinach, thawed and drained
1 cup gorgonzola crumbles
1 teaspoon ground black pepper

1. Mix all ingredients in medium bowl. Oil the slow-cooker stoneware.

2. Place batter in the **CROCK-POT®** slow cooker; cook on HIGH, covered, for 1½ hours. Sprinkle top with paprika for more colorful crust, if desired.

Note: Cook only on HIGH setting for proper crust and texture.

Crock Pot Stoneware Slow Cooker Tip

Gorgonzola, a delicious blue cheese from Italy, is available in wedges and already crumbled.

Spinach Gorgonzola Corn Bread

Jambalaya

MAKES 6 SERVINGS

PREP TIME: 10 MINUTES
COOK TIME: 6 TO 7 HOURS (LOW) • 3½ TO 4 HOURS (HIGH)

2½ to 3 pounds chicken pieces, skinned if desired
1 can (14½ ounces) diced tomatoes
1 can (14½ ounces) chicken broth
1 green bell pepper, chopped
2 cups **French's**® French Fried Onions
¼ cup **Frank's**® **RedHot**® Cayenne Pepper Sauce
2 cloves garlic, chopped
2 teaspoons Old Bay® seafood seasoning
1½ teaspoons dried oregano leaves
¾ teaspoon salt
½ teaspoon ground black pepper
1 cup uncooked regular rice
1 pound shrimp, peeled and deveined

1. Combine the chicken, tomatoes, chicken broth, green pepper, 1 cup **French's**® French Fried Onions, **Frank's**® **RedHot**® Cayenne Pepper Sauce, garlic, seafood seasoning, oregano, salt and pepper in the **CROCK-POT**® slow cooker. Cover and cook on LOW for 4 to 5 hours or on HIGH for 2 to 2½ hours.

2. Stir in the rice. Cook on LOW for 2 hours or on HIGH for 1 hour or until rice is cooked and all liquid is absorbed.

3. Turn **CROCK-POT**® slow cooker to HIGH. Add shrimp. Cover and cook 30 minutes or until shrimp are pink. Arrange jambalaya on serving platter. Sprinkle with remaining 1 cup French Fried Onions.

Jambalaya

Campbell's® Golden Mushroom Pork & Apples

MAKES 8 SERVINGS

PREP TIME: 10 MINUTES
COOK TIME: 8 TO 9 HOURS (LOW) • 4 TO 5 HOURS (HIGH)

2 cans (10¾ ounces each) **CAMPBELL'S®** Condensed Golden
    Mushroom Soup
½ cup water
1 tablespoon brown sugar
1 tablespoon Worcestershire sauce
1 teaspoon dried thyme leaves, crushed
4 large Granny Smith apples, sliced (about 4 cups)
2 large onions, sliced (about 2 cups)
8 boneless pork chops, ¾ inch thick

1. Mix soup, water, brown sugar, Worcestershire and thyme in the **CROCK-POT®** slow cooker. Add apples, onions and pork.

2. Cover and cook on LOW for 8 to 9 hours or on HIGH for 4 to 5 hours or until pork is tender.

Is Cooking With Rival®!

The sweet-tart flavor of Granny Smith apples complements pork. For a more attractive appearance, leave the skins on the apples.

Campbell's® Golden Mushroom Pork & Apples

 **AMERICAN CLASSICS**

Fresh Herbed Turkey Breast

MAKES 8 SERVINGS

PREP TIME: 5 MINUTES
COOK TIME: 8 TO 10 HOURS (LOW) • 4 TO 5 HOURS (HIGH)

 2 tablespoons butter, softened
 ¼ cup fresh sage leaves, minced
 ¼ cup fresh tarragon leaves, minced
 1 clove garlic, minced
 1 teaspoon black pepper
 ½ teaspoon salt
 1 (4-pound) split turkey breast
 1½ tablespoons cornstarch

1. Mix together the softened butter, sage, tarragon, garlic, pepper and salt. Rub the butter mixture all over the turkey breast.

2. Place the turkey breast in the **CROCK-POT**® slow cooker. Cover; cook on LOW for 8 to 10 hours or on HIGH for 4 to 5 hours or until turkey is no longer pink in the center.

3. Remove the turkey breast from the stoneware. Turn the slow cooker to HIGH; slowly whisk in the cornstarch to thicken the juices. When the sauce is thick and smooth, pour over the turkey breast. Slice to serve.

Fresh Herbed Turkey Breast

Cajun Chicken and Shrimp Creole

MAKES 6 SERVINGS

PREP TIME: 12 TO 15 MINUTES
COOK TIME: 8 TO 10 HOURS (LOW) • 4 TO 5 HOURS (HIGH)

1 **pound skinless chicken thighs**
1 **red bell pepper, chopped**
1 **large onion, chopped**
1 **stalk celery, diced**
1 **can (15 ounces) stewed tomatoes, undrained and chopped**
1 **clove garlic, minced**
1 **tablespoon sugar**
1 **teaspoon paprika**
1 **teaspoon Cajun seasoning**
1 **teaspoon salt**
1 **teaspoon black pepper**
1 **pound shelled shrimp, deveined and cleaned**
1 **tablespoon fresh lemon juice**
  Louisiana-style hot sauce to taste
1 **cup prepared quick-cooking rice**

1. Place the chicken thighs in the **CROCK-POT®** slow cooker. Add the bell pepper, onion, celery, tomatoes with juice, garlic, sugar, paprika, Cajun seasoning, salt and pepper.

2. Cover; cook on LOW for 8 to 10 hours or on HIGH for 4 to 5 hours.

3. In the last hour of cooking, add the shrimp, lemon juice and hot sauce. Serve over the hot rice.

Cajun Chicken and Shrimp Creole

Pork Loin with Sherry and Red Onions

MAKES 8 SERVINGS

PREP TIME: 15 MINUTES
COOK TIME: 8 TO 10 HOURS (LOW) • 5 TO 6 HOURS (HIGH)

3 large red onions, thinly sliced
1 cup pearl onions, blanched and peeled
1 tablespoon unsalted butter or margarine
2½ pounds boneless pork loin, tied
½ teaspoon salt
½ teaspoon freshly ground black pepper
½ cup cooking sherry
2 tablespoons chopped Italian parsley
1½ tablespoons cornstarch
2 tablespoons water

1. Cook the red onions and pearl onions in the butter in a medium skillet until soft.

2. Rub the pork loin with salt and pepper and place in the **CROCK-POT®** slow cooker. Add the cooked onions, sherry and parsley. Cover; cook on LOW for 8 to 10 hours or on HIGH for 5 to 6 hours.

3. Remove the pork loin from the stoneware; let stand 15 minutes before slicing.

4. Combine the cornstarch and water; add to the juice in the stoneware to thicken the sauce. Serve the pork loin with the onions and sherry sauce.

Pork Loin with Sherry and Red Onions

Campbell's® Lemon Chicken

MAKES 8 SERVINGS

PREP TIME: 5 MINUTES
COOK TIME: 7 TO 8 HOURS (LOW) • 4 TO 5 HOURS (HIGH)

**2 cans (10¾ ounces each) CAMPBELL'S® Condensed Cream of
Chicken Soup *or* 98% Fat Free Cream of Chicken Soup**

½ cup water

¼ cup lemon juice

2 teaspoons Dijon-style mustard

1½ teaspoons garlic powder

8 large carrots, thickly sliced (about 6 cups)

8 skinless, boneless chicken breast halves (about 2 pounds)

8 cups hot cooked egg noodles

Grated Parmesan cheese

1. Mix soup, water, lemon juice, mustard, garlic powder and carrots in the **CROCK-POT®** slow cooker. Add chicken and turn to coat.

2. Cover and cook on LOW for 7 to 8 hours or on HIGH for 4 to 5 hours or until chicken is done.

3. Serve over noodles. Sprinkle with cheese.

Campbell's® Creamy Chicken & Wild Rice

MAKES 8 SERVINGS

PREP TIME: 5 MINUTES
COOK TIME: 7 TO 8 HOURS (LOW) • 4 TO 5 HOURS (HIGH)

**2 cans (10¾ ounces each) CAMPBELL'S® Condensed Cream of
    Chicken Soup *or* 98% Fat Free Cream of Chicken Soup**
1½ cups water
1 package (6 ounces) seasoned long grain and wild rice mix
4 large carrots, thickly sliced (about 3 cups)
8 skinless, boneless chicken breast halves (about 2 pounds)

1. Mix soup, water, rice and carrots in the **CROCK-POT®** slow cooker. Add chicken and turn to coat.

2. Cover and cook on LOW for 7 to 8 hours or on HIGH for 4 to 5 hours or until chicken and rice are done.

Campbell's® Savory Pot Roast

MAKES 7 TO 8 SERVINGS

PREP TIME: 10 MINUTES
COOK TIME: 8 TO 9 HOURS (LOW) • 4 TO 5 HOURS (HIGH)

**1 can (10¾ ounces) CAMPBELL'S® Condensed Cream of Mushroom
    Soup *or* 98% Fat Free Cream of Mushroom Soup**
1 pouch CAMPBELL'S® Dry Onion Soup and Recipe Mix
6 medium potatoes, cut into 1-inch pieces (about 6 cups)
6 medium carrots, thickly sliced (about 3 cups)
1 (3½- to 4-pound) boneless chuck pot roast, trimmed

1. Mix soup, soup mix, potatoes and carrots in the **CROCK-POT®** slow cooker. Add roast and turn to coat.

2. Cover and cook on LOW for 8 to 9 hours or on HIGH for 4 to 5 hours or until roast and vegetables are done.

Sweets &
DES

SERTS

Cran-Apple Orange Conserve

MAKES ABOUT 5 CUPS

PREP TIME: 12 MINUTES
COOK TIME: 6 HOURS (LOW) • 3 TO 3½ HOURS (HIGH)

2 medium oranges
5 large tart apples, peeled, cored and chopped
2 cups sugar
1½ cups fresh cranberries
1 tablespoon grated fresh lemon peel

1. Remove a thin slice from both ends of both oranges for easier chopping. Finely chop unpeeled oranges and remove any seeds. You should have about 2 cups of chopped orange.

2. Combine oranges, apples, sugar, cranberries and lemon peel in the **CROCK-POT**® slow cooker. Cover; cook on LOW for 4 hours or on HIGH for 2 hours. Slightly crush fruit with potato masher.

3. Cook, uncovered, on LOW for 2 hours or on HIGH for 1 to 1½ hours or until very thick, stirring occasionally to prevent sticking. Cool at least 2 hours.

4. Serve with pound cake, waffles or pancakes.

Serving Suggestion: Fruit conserve can also be served with roast pork or poultry.

Brownie Bottoms

MAKES 6 SERVINGS

PREP TIME: 12 MINUTES
COOK TIME: 1½ HOURS (HIGH)

½ **cup brown sugar**
¾ **cup water**
1 **tablespoon unsweetened cocoa powder**
2½ **cups packaged brownie mix**
1 **package (2¾ ounces) instant chocolate pudding mix**
½ **cup milk chocolate chip morsels**
2 **eggs, beaten**
3 **tablespoons butter or margarine, melted**

1. Lightly grease the **CROCK-POT**® slow cooker stoneware with nonstick cooking spray. In a small saucepan, combine the brown sugar, water and cocoa powder; bring to a boil.

2. Combine the brownie mix, pudding mix, morsels, eggs and butter in a medium bowl; stir until well blended. Spread the batter into the stoneware; pour the boiling sugar mixture over the batter. Cover; cook on HIGH for 1½ hours.

3. Turn off the heat and let stand for 30 minutes. Serve warm.

Serving Suggestion: Serve this warm chocolate dessert with whipped cream or ice cream.

Brownie Bottoms

Steamed Pumpkin Cake

MAKES 12 SERVINGS

PREP TIME: 15 MINUTES
COOK TIME: 3 TO 3½ HOURS (HIGH)

1½ **cups all-purpose flour**
1½ **teaspoons baking powder**
1½ **teaspoons baking soda**
   1 **teaspoon ground cinnamon**
   ½ **teaspoon salt**
   ¼ **teaspoon ground cloves**
   ½ **cup unsalted butter, melted**
   2 **cups packed light brown sugar**
   3 **eggs, beaten**
   1 **can (15 ounces) pumpkin**
      Sweetened whipped cream (optional)

1. Grease 2½-quart soufflé dish or baking pan that fits into the **CROCK-POT®** slow cooker stoneware. Slow cooker baking pans can be purchased by visiting www.crock-pot.com.

2. Combine flour, baking powder, baking soda, cinnamon, salt and cloves in medium bowl; set aside.

3. Beat butter, brown sugar and eggs in large bowl with electric mixer on medium speed until creamy. Beat in pumpkin. Stir in flour mixture. Spoon batter into prepared soufflé dish.

4. Fill stoneware with 1 inch hot water. Make foil handles using technique described below to allow for easy removal of soufflé dish. Place soufflé dish into stoneware. Cover; cook on HIGH for 3 to 3½ hours or until wooden toothpick inserted into center comes out clean.

5. Use foil handles to lift dish from stoneware. Cool 15 minutes. Invert cake onto serving platter. Cut into wedges and serve with dollop of whipped cream, if desired.

Foil Handles: Tear off three 18×2-inch strips of heavy-duty foil or use regular foil folded to double thickness. Crisscross foil strips in spoke design and place soufflé dish on center of strips. Pull foil strips up and over dish.

Serving Suggestion: Enhance this old-fashioned dense cake with a topping of sautéed apples or pear slices, or a scoop of pumpkin ice cream.

Banana Nut Bread

MAKES 6 SERVINGS

PREP TIME: 15 MINUTES
COOK TIME: 2 TO 3 HOURS (HIGH)

⅓ **cup butter or margarine**
⅔ **cup sugar**
2 **eggs, well beaten**
2 **tablespoons dark corn syrup**
3 **ripe bananas, well mashed**
1¾ **cups all-purpose flour**
2 **teaspoons baking powder**
½ **teaspoon salt**
¼ **teaspoon baking soda**
½ **cup chopped walnuts**

1. Grease and flour the inside of the **CROCK-POT**® slow cooker stoneware. Cream the butter in a large bowl with an electric mixer until fluffy. Slowly add the sugar, eggs, corn syrup and mashed bananas. Beat until smooth.

2. Sift together the flour, baking powder, salt and baking soda in a small bowl. Slowly beat the flour mixture into the creamed mixture. Add the walnuts and mix well. Pour into the stoneware. Cover; cook on HIGH for 2 to 3 hours.

3. Let cool, then turn bread out onto the serving platter.

Note: Banana nut bread has always been a favorite way to use up those overripe bananas. Not only is it delicious, but it also freezes well for future use.

Homestyle Apple Brown Betty

MAKES 8 SERVINGS

PREP TIME: 15 MINUTES
COOK TIME: 3 TO 4 HOURS (LOW) • 2 HOURS (HIGH)

**6 cups of your favorite cooking apples, peeled, cored and
    cut into eighths**
1 cup bread crumbs
1 teaspoon ground cinnamon
1 teaspoon ground nutmeg
⅛ teaspoon salt
¾ cup packed brown sugar
½ cup butter or margarine, melted
¼ cup finely chopped walnuts

1. Lightly grease the **CROCK-POT®** slow cooker stoneware. Place the apples on the bottom of the stoneware.

2. Combine the bread crumbs, cinnamon, nutmeg, salt, brown sugar, butter and walnuts. Spread over the apples in the stoneware.

3. Cover; cook on LOW for 3 to 4 hours or on HIGH for 2 hours.

Homestyle Apple Brown Betty

METRIC CONVERSION CHART

VOLUME MEASUREMENTS (dry)

$^1/_8$ teaspoon = 0.5 mL
$^1/_4$ teaspoon = 1 mL
$^1/_2$ teaspoon = 2 mL
$^3/_4$ teaspoon = 4 mL
1 teaspoon = 5 mL
1 tablespoon = 15 mL
2 tablespoons = 30 mL
$^1/_4$ cup = 60 mL
$^1/_3$ cup = 75 mL
$^1/_2$ cup = 125 mL
$^2/_3$ cup = 150 mL
$^3/_4$ cup = 175 mL
1 cup = 250 mL
2 cups = 1 pint = 500 mL
3 cups = 750 mL
4 cups = 1 quart = 1 L

VOLUME MEASUREMENTS (fluid)

1 fluid ounce (2 tablespoons) = 30 mL
4 fluid ounces ($^1/_2$ cup) = 125 mL
8 fluid ounces (1 cup) = 250 mL
12 fluid ounces (1$^1/_2$ cups) = 375 mL
16 fluid ounces (2 cups) = 500 mL

WEIGHTS (mass)

$^1/_2$ ounce = 15 g
1 ounce = 30 g
3 ounces = 90 g
4 ounces = 120 g
8 ounces = 225 g
10 ounces = 285 g
12 ounces = 360 g
16 ounces = 1 pound = 450 g

DIMENSIONS

$^1/_{16}$ inch = 2 mm
$^1/_8$ inch = 3 mm
$^1/_4$ inch = 6 mm
$^1/_2$ inch = 1.5 cm
$^3/_4$ inch = 2 cm
1 inch = 2.5 cm

OVEN TEMPERATURES

250°F = 120°C
275°F = 140°C
300°F = 150°C
325°F = 160°C
350°F = 180°C
375°F = 190°C
400°F = 200°C
425°F = 220°C
450°F = 230°C

BAKING PAN SIZES

Utensil	Size in Inches/Quarts	Metric Volume	Size in Centimeters
Baking or Cake Pan (square or rectangular)	8×8×2	2 L	20×20×5
	9×9×2	2.5 L	23×23×5
	12×8×2	3 L	30×20×5
	13×9×2	3.5 L	33×23×5
Loaf Pan	8×4×3	1.5 L	20×10×7
	9×5×3	2 L	23×13×7
Round Layer Cake Pan	8×1½	1.2 L	20×4
	9×1½	1.5 L	23×4
Pie Plate	8×1¼	750 mL	20×3
	9×1¼	1 L	23×3
Baking Dish or Casserole	1 quart	1 L	—
	1½ quart	1.5 L	—
	2 quart	2 L	—